Handy Louisiana Genealogy Handbook

I0450613

By G.L.Morris

ISBN-13: 978-1506184562

ISBN-10: 1506184561

Table of Contents

Notes

Genealogical Research in Louisiana

Tracing your family history in Louisiana can be a fascinating trip through time. Louisiana was inhabited at one time by the French, Spanish, Mexicans, British, and of course Native Americans. As such there is a large cultural diversity in the genealogical records available for the state, some to be found in the archives of foreign countries.

Locating the relevant genealogical records you'll need to find your ancestors however can be a frustrating experience, especially if you need to look in overseas archives. To help you avoid those frustrations when tracing your Louisiana ancestry, we'll show you which records you'll need, and help you to understand:

1. What they are
2. Where to find them
3. How to use them

These records can be found both online and off, so we'll introduce you to online websites, indexes and databases, as well as brick-and-mortar repositories and other institutions that will help with your research in Louisiana. So that you will have a more comprehensive understanding of these records, we have provided a brief history of the "Pelican State" to illustrate what type of records may have been generated during specific time periods. That information will assist you in pinpointing times and locations on which to focus the search for your Louisiana ancestors and their records.

A Brief History of Louisiana

Louisiana's history is filled with intrigue, adventure, and ethnic culture. Beginning in 1541 when Hernando de Soto claimed the area for Spain, Louisiana was ruled under ten different flags. The region was subsequently claimed by France, and was at one time or another subject to the Lone Star flag of the Republic of West Florida, the Union Jack of Great Britain, and the fifteen stars of the United States. Six weeks before joining the Confederacy, Louisiana became an independent republic, but joined the southern cause at the outbreak of the Civil War.

Before that, in 1803, Louisiana had joined the United States as a result of the Louisiana Purchase. Because the region was so vital to the security and trade of America, President Thomas Jefferson negotiated the purchase of land that would include the future states of Arkansas, Iowa, Louisiana, Missouri, Nebraska, North Dakota, Oklahoma, and South Dakota.

With the land acquired by the Louisiana Purchase, the sixe of the United States nearly doubled, propelling it forward as a world power. Louisiana was very much a trading and financial center during its early days, and its fertile land which encouraged the growth of crops such as sugar, indigo, and cotton, made it one of the |United States' richest regions. The owners of Louisiana plantations were at the time some of the richest men in the world.

The Civil War shattered the plantation economy, but the state managed to maintain its status as a powerful agricultural force. Sulphur was discovered in 1869, and in 1901, the first oil strike occurred on the "Mamou Prairie" in the community of Evangeline near Jennings. Coupled with the success of a forestry program, Louisiana prospered and went on to become a major producer of natural gas and oil, and a major center for the production pf petrochemicals and oil refining.

Important Dates in Louisiana History

- **1541** – Claimed by Spain
- **1699** – France establishes its first settlements.
- **1712** – Chartered as a province of France
- **1714** – City of Natchitoches founded.
- **1720** – Becomes Crown Colony of France
- **1763** - Ceded to Spain
- **1769** – Spanish military forces take possession of the colony and abolish French civil law
- **1800** – Ceded back to France
- **1803** – Becomes part of the United States in the Louisiana Purchas
- **1804** – Organized as US Territory of Orleans and the District of Louisiana
- **1805** – Louisiana Territory reorganized
- **1808** – Adopts its own civil code that contained elements of Spanish, French, and English law
- **1812** - Statehood.
- **1861** – Secedes from Union
- **1868** – Readmitted to Union

Famous Battles Fought in Louisiana

Several Civil War battles were fought in Louisiana, and the War of 1812 brought the Battle of New Orleans. Below you fill find a list of the major battles that took place on Louisiana soil along with links to websites where you can learn more about them.These battle accounts can be very effective in uncovering the military records of your ancestor. They can tell you what regiments fought in which battles, and often include the names and ranks of many officers and enlisted men.

Battle of Donaldsonville, 1863 – Civil War

Battle of Donaldsonville, 1863:
http://americancivilwar.com/statepic/la/la013.html

Battle of Baton Rouge, 1862 – Civil War

Battle of Baton Rouge, 1862:
http://www.exploresouthernhistory.com/batonrougebattle.html

Battle of St. John's Bluff, 1862 – Civil War

Battle of St. John's Bluff, 1862:
http://www.cr.nps.gov/HPS/abpp/battles/fl003.htm

Battle of Georgia Landing, 1862 – Civil War

Battle of Georgia Landing, 1862
http://www.americancivilwar.com/statepic/la/la005.html

Battle of Kock's Plantation, 1862

Battle of Kock's Plantation, 1862:
http://www.nps.gov/hps/abpp/battles/la015.htm

Battle of New Orleans, 1815 – War of 1812

Battle of New Orleans, 1815:
http://www.eighteentwelve.ca/?q=eng/Topic/59

Common Louisiana Genealogical Issues and Resources to Overcome Them

Boundary Changes: Boundary changes are a common obstacle when researching Louisiana ancestors. You could be searching for an ancestor's record in one county when in fact it is stored in a different one due to historical county boundary changes. The **Atlas of Historical County Boundaries** can help you to overcome that problem. It provides a chronological listing of every boundary change that has occurred in the history of Louisiana.

Atlas of Historical County Boundaries:
http://publications.newberry.org/ahcbp/documents/LA_Consolidated _Chronology.htm#Consolidated_Chronology

Name Changes: Surname changes, variations, and misspellings can complicate genealogical research. It is important to check all spelling variations. Soundex, a program that indexes names by sound, is a useful first step, but you can't rely on it completely as some name variations result in different Soundex codes. The surnames could be different, but the first name may be different too. You can also find records filed under initials, middle names, and nicknames as well, so you will need to **get creative with surname variations** and spellings in order to cover all the possibilities. For help with surname variations read our instructional article on **How to Use Soundex**.

get creative with surname variations:
http://obituarieshelp.org/blog/?p=634

How to Use Soundex: http://obituarieshelp.org/blog/?p=505

Louisiana Genealogical Organizations and Archives

Genealogical resources include not only records, but the organizations that house them, or can direct you to them. These institutions include: *Archives, Libraries, Genealogical Societies, Family History Centers, Universities, Churches, and Museums.*

Following are links to their websites, their physical addresses, and a summary of the records you can find there.

Archives and Libraries

Louisiana State Archives – census indexes, immigration schedules, church records, colonial documents, passenger manifests for the Port of New Orleans, assessment records, military service records, Confederate Pension Applications and records from the State Land Office

3851 Essen Lane
P.O. Box 94125
Baton Rouge, LA 70804-9125
Tel: 225.922.1000
Fax: 225.922.0433

Louisiana State Archives:
http://www.sos.la.gov/HistoricalResources/ResearchHistoricalRecords/Pages/default.aspx

National Archives at Fort Worth, Texas - census records, land records, military records, passenger lists, immigration and naturalization records, Native and African American records

1400 John Burgess Drive
Fort Worth, Texas 76140
Tel: 817-551-2051
Fax: 817-551-2034
E-mail: ftworth.archives@nara.gov

National Archives at Fort Worth, Texas:
http://www.archives.gov/fort-worth/

New Orleans Notarial Archives – Searchable online index of notary records which include Slave emancipations, property records, bonds, slave sales records, wills, mortgages, estate records and many other notary records dating from 1735 to July 1970

Notarial Archives Division Research Center
1340 Poydras Street, Suite 360
New Orleans, LA 70112
Telephone: (504) 407-0106
Fax: (504) 680-9607

Website: http://www.notarialarchives.org/research.htm

The Historic New Orleans Collection (HNOC) historical maps and photographs, African American military records, German community records, city directories, records from the French National Archives, records of the Spanish and Cuban National Archives, historical newspapers, manuscripts

Williams Research Center
533 Royal Street
New Orleans, LA 70130

Website: http://www.hnoc.org/collections/research_subjects.html

Tulane University Louisiana Research Collection - Colonial Louisiana, Civil War, Jewish studies, medical history, social welfare, Southern literature, Louisiana politics, waterways, and women's studies.

Room 202 Jones Hall
6801 Freret Street
Tulane University
New Orleans, LA 70118
Phone: 504-865-5685
Fax: 504-865-5671
Email: larc@tulane.edu

Website: http://larc.tulane.edu/

Louisiana Genealogical and Historical Societies

Genealogical and historical societies have access to extensive catalogues of genealogical data. They are also able to offer expert guidance for genealogical researchers. Many members are professional genealogists who are most willing to share their expertise in finding ancestors.

The Louisiana State Historical Center (Appointment required to access records) – Colonial-era manuscripts dating from 1584-present, maps, Louisiana Colonial Judicial Records of both the French Superior Council (1714-1769) and the Spanish Judiciary (1769-1803), historical newspapers

Louisiana State Museum
400 Esplanade Avenue
New Orleans, LA 70116

For research appointments contact:
Erin Kinchen, Reading Room Attendant
Phone: 504-568-3659
Email: ekinchen@crt.la.gov

The Louisiana State Historical Center:
http://www.crt.state.la.us/museum/collections/historical_center/

Central Louisiana Genealogical Society – Bible records, wills, cemetery indexes, diaries, census

P. O. Box 12206
Alexandria, Louisiana 71301
Central Louisiana Genealogical Society:
http://www.rootsweb.ancestry.com/~laclgs/?cj=1&netid=cj&o_xid=0001231185&o_lid=0001231185&o_sch=Affiliate+External

Jewish Genealogical Society of New Orleans – Jewish burial records, histories and other resources related to Jewish genealogy

P.O. Box 7811
Metairie, LA 70010
Tel: (504)836-2720
Fax: (504)836-2722
Email: jkarno@karnovsky.co

Jewish Genealogical Society of New Orleans:
http://www.jewishgen.org/jgsno/

German - Acadian Coast Historical and Genealogical Society – miscellaneous resources for German, Cajun, French, and Acadian genealogy research

P.O. Box 3086
LaPlace, Louisiana 70069-3086

German - Acadian Coast Historical and Genealogical Society:
http://germanacadiancoast.com/

Additional Louisiana Genealogical Resources

<u>Louisiana Mailing Lists</u>

Mailing lists are internet based facilities that use email to distribute a single message to all who subscribe to it. When information on a particular surname, new records, or any other important genealogy information related to the mailing list topic becomes available, the subscribers are alerted to it. Joining a mailing list is an excellent way to stay up to date on Louisiana genealogy research topics. Rootsweb have an extensive listing of **Louisiana Mailing Lists** on a variety of topics.

Louisiana Mailing Lists:
http://lists.rootsweb.ancestry.com/index/usa/LA/misc.html

<u>Louisiana Message Boards</u>

A message board is another internet based facility where people can post questions about a specific genealogy topic and have it answered by other genealogists. If you have questions about a surname, record type, or research topic, you can post your question and other researchers and genealogists will help you with the answer. Be sure to check back regularly, as the answers are not emailed to you. The Louisiana Message Boards at **Rootsweb** are completely free to use.

Rootsweb:
http://boards.rootsweb.com/localities.northam.usa.states/mb.ashx

Louisiana Newspapers and Periodicals

Many genealogy periodicals and historical newspapers contain reprinted copies of family genealogies, transcripts of family Bible records, information about local records and archives, census indexes, church records, queries, land records, obituaries, court records, cemetery records, and wills. The following sites have historical Louisiana newspapers and periodicals that you can search online or on-site.

The Louisiana State Historical Center (Appointment required to access records) – late nineteenth and early twentieth-century Louisiana newspapers, French newspapers published in New Orleans from the early 1700s onwards

Louisiana State Museum
400 Esplanade Avenue
New Orleans, LA 70116

For research appointments contact:
Erin Kinchen, Reading Room Attendant
Phone: 504-568-3659
Email: ekinchen@crt.la.gov

The Louisiana State Historical Center:
http://www.crt.state.la.us/museum/collections/historical_center/Newspapers.aspx

GenealogyBank.com – free searchable database of Louisiana newspaper archives, 1805–1988

GenealogyBank.com:
http://www.genealogybank.com/gbnk/newspapers/explore/USA/Louisiana/

Library of Congress Digital Newspaper Directory – free searchable database of historical U.S. newspapers dating from 1690-present

Library of Congress Digital Newspaper Directory:
http://chroniclingamerica.loc.gov/search/titles/

The Online Books Page – links to historical books and periodicals available for viewing online, dating from mid-16th century

The Online Books Page:
http://onlinebooks.library.upenn.edu/webbin/book//browse?type=lcsubc&key=Louisiana%20--%20History%20--%20Periodicals

NewspaperArchive.com – largest online database of historical newspapers in the world.

NewspaperArchive.com: http://newspaperarchive.com/

Historical Louisiana Maps and Gazetteers

Maps are an integral part of genealogical research. They help us to locate landmarks, towns, cities, parishes, states, provinces, waterways and roads and streets. They also help us to determine when and where boundary changes might have taken place, and give us a visualization of the area we're researching in.

For locating place names, a gazetteer is the best possible resource for any genealogist. Gazetteers are also sometimes called "place name dictionaries", and can help you to locate the area in which you need to conduct research. Below are links to the maps and gazetteers for research in Louisiana.

Peabody GNIS Service – Louisiana:
http://peabody.research.yale.edu/cgi-bin/Query.GNIS?ST=Louisiana&SU=1

Color Landform Atlas – Louisiana:
http://fermi.jhuapl.edu/states/la_0.html

1985 U.S. Atlas: http://www.livgenmi.com/1895/LA/

Louisiana Hometown Locator:
http://louisiana.hometownlocator.com/

Louisiana City Directories

.

City directories are similar to telephone directories in that they list the residents of a particular area. The difference though is what is important to genealogists, and that is they pre-date telephone directories. You can find an ancestor's information such as their street address, place of employment, occupation, or the name of their spouse. A one-stop-shop for finding city directories in Louisiana is the **Louisiana Online Historical Directories** which contains a listing of every available historical directory related to Louisiana.

Louisiana Online Historical Directories:
https://sites.google.com/site/onlinedirectorysite/Home/usa/la

New Orleans Public Library - New Orleans city directories for most years since 1805.

New Orleans Public Library:
http://nutrias.org/info/louinfo/citydir.htm

Fold3.com -New Orleans City Directories 1861 and 1866-1923 (3 yrs. missing)

Fold3.com: http://www.fold3.com/s.php#t=122

State Library of Louisiana Louisiana Collection - Newspapers from major Louisiana cities in print, on microfilm and in electronic format

701 North 4th Street,
Baton Rouge, LA 70802
Phone: (225) 342-4913
Fax: (225) 219-4804

State Library of Louisiana Louisiana Collection:
http://www.state.lib.la.us/library-collections/louisiana-collection

Louisiana Genealogical Records

Birth, Death, Marriage and Divorce Records – Also known as vital records, birth, death, and marriage certificates are the most basic, yet most important records attached to your ancestor. The reason for their importance is that they not only place your ancestor in a specific place at a definite time, but potentially connect the individual to other relatives. Below is a list of repositories and websites where you can find Louisiana vital records

Louisiana Vital Records State Department of Health has birth records less than 100 years old, marriage records less than 50 years old, and death records less than 50 years old. They can be ordered by writing to:

Office of Public Health
Vital Records Registry
P.O. Box 60630
New Orleans, LA 70160

Louisiana Vital Records State Department of Health:
http://www.cdc.gov/nchs/w2w/Louisiana.htm

Older death, birth, and marriage record indexes for Louisiana (dating from late 18th century) can be browsed online at the **Louisiana Vital Records Index** webpage courtesy of the Louisiana State Archives. Copies can be ordered for $5 from:

Louisiana State Archives
Louisiana Secretary of State
P.O. Box 94125
Baton Rouge, LA 70804-9125

Louisiana Vital Records Index:
http://www.sos.la.gov/HistoricalResources/ResearchHistoricalRecords/Pages/OnlinePublicVitalRecordsIndex.aspx

Divorce records must be obtained from **Louisiana Clerks of Court**.

Louisiana Clerks of Court:
http://www.laclerksofcourt.org/clerksofcourt.htm

Family Search has the following indexes that can be searched for free online:

Louisiana, Births and Christenings, 1811-1830; 1854-1934 link to: https://familysearch.org/search/collection/1674847

Louisiana Deaths Index, 1850-1875, 1894-1956 link to: https://familysearch.org/search/collection/1609793

Louisiana Marriages, 1816-1906 link to: https://familysearch.org/search/collection/1674881

Louisiana Parish Marriages, 1837-1957 link to: https://familysearch.org/search/collection/1807364

<u>Census Reports</u>

Census records are among the most important genealogical documents for placing your ancestor in a particular place at a specific time. Like BDM records, they can also lead you to other ancestors, particularly those who were living under the authority of the head of household.

Federal census records for Louisiana exist from 1810 through 1930, with the exception of the 1890 census which was destroyed. They can be found in the following repositories:

New Orleans Public Library's Louisiana Division & City Archives - 1810 – 1930, 1850 – 1880 (Mortality Schedules), 1850 – 1860 (Slave Schedules), 1890 (Ascension Parish only), 1890 (Special Census of Union Veterans and Widows of Union Veterans)

219 Loyola Ave
New Orleans, LA 70112
Tel: 504-529-7323

New Orleans Public Library's Louisiana Division & City Archives: http://nutrias.org/guides/genguide/censusrecords.htm

The **Free Census Project** has transcribed many Louisiana indexes and new material is added daily

Free Census Project: http://usgwcensus.org/cenfiles/la.htm

Access Genealogy – Louisiana county census records from 1810

Access Genealogy :
http://www.accessgenealogy.com/census/Louisiana-census-records.htm

African American Census Schedules Online – slave schedules, mortality schedules, slave-owners census

African American Census Schedules Online:
http://www.afrigeneas.com/aacensus/ga/

Native Americans in Census Records (US National Archives)

Native Americans in Census Records:
http://www.archives.gov/research/census/native-americans/

Louisiana Church Records

Church and synagogue records are a valuable resource, especially for baptisms, marriages, and burials that took place before 1900. You will need to at least have an idea of your ancestor's religious denomination, and in most cases you will have to visit a brick and mortar establishment to view them.

Most church records are kept by the individual church, although in some denominations, records are placed in a regional archive or maintained at the diocesan level. Local Historical Societies are sometimes the repository for the state's older church records. Below are links archives that maintain church records, as well as a few databases that can be viewed online.

The **Family History Library** contains many church records from a variety of denominations on microfilm.

Family History Library:
http://familysearch.org/learn/wiki/en/Family_History_Library

New Orleans Public Library's Louisiana Division & City Archives – large collection of multi-denominational parish registers that include baptisms, marriages, and funerals dating from colonial times

219 Loyola Ave
New Orleans, LA 70112
Tel: 504-529-7323

New Orleans Public Library's Louisiana Division & City Archives : http://nutrias.org/guides/genguide/churchrecords.htm

Central Repositories for Denominational Records

Most of the records of individual denominations are kept in central repositories. Below is a list of the major congregational archives for Louisiana with links to their websites, physical addresses, and contact information.

Roman Catholic

Diocese of Alexandria
4400 Coliseum Boulevard
Alexandria, LA 71303
Phone: (318) 445-2401
Fax: (318) 448-6121

Diocese of Alexandria: http://www.diocesealex.org/archives

Diocese of Baton Rouge Archives
1800 South Acadian Thruway
Baton Rouge, LA 70808
Phone: (504) 387-0561
Fax: (504) 336-8789

Mailing Address:
P.O. Box 2028
Baton Rouge, LA 70821-2028

Diocese of Baton Rouge Archives:
http://www.diobr.org/index.php?option=com_phocadownload&view
=category&id=36:archives-documents&Itemid=5

Diocese of Houma-Thibodaux Archives
205 Audubon Avenue
Thibodaux, LA 70301
Phone: (985) 446-2383
E-Mail: kallemand@htdiocese.org

Diocese of Houma-Thibodaux Archives:
http://www.htdiocese.org/Default.aspx?alias=www.htdiocese.org/archives

Diocese of Lafayette
1408 Carmel Dr.
Lafayette, LA 70501
Phone: (337) 261-5652

Mailing address:
P.O. Box 3387
Lafayette, LA 70502-3387

Diocese of Lafayette: http://www.diolaf.org/

Diocese of Lake Charles Archives
414 Iris Street
Lake Charles, LA 70601
Phone: (337) 439-7400

Diocese of Lake Charles Archives:
http://live.lcdiocese.org/administration/43-offices-and-agencies/37-deacon-george-stearns.html

Archdiocese of New Orleans Archives
7887 Walmsley Avenue
New Orleans, LA 70125-3496
Phone: (504) 861-9521
Fax: (504) 866-2906

Archdiocese of New Orleans Archives: http://www.archdiocese-no.org/archives/index.php

Archives of the Diocese of Shreveport
3500 Fairfield Avenue
Shreveport, LA 71104
Phone: (318) 868-4441

Archives of the Diocese of Shreveport:
http://www.dioshpt.org/archives/archives.htm

Baptist

Southern Baptist Historical Commission and Archives
Southern Baptist Convention
901 Commerce Street
Nashville, TN 37203-3630
Phone: (615) 244-0344
Fax: (615) 782-4821

Southern Baptist Historical Commission and Archives:
http://www.sbhla.org/links.htm

Church of Jesus Christ of Latter-day Saints (Mormons)
Early Mormon Church records for Louisiana can be found on film
located at the LDS Family History Library in Salt Lake City and can
be searched via the **Family History Library Catalog**

Family History Library Catalog:
https://familysearch.org/eng/Library/FHLC/frameset_fhlc.asp

Methodist

Centenary College of Louisiana
Magale Library, Cline Room
Shreveport, LA 71134-1188
Phone: (318) 869-5170
Fax: (318) 869-5004

Mailing Address:
P.O. Box 41188
Shreveport, LA 71134-1188

Centenary College of Louisiana: http://www.centenary.edu/

Lutheran

Earl K. Long Library—Archives and Manuscripts Division
University of New Orleans
Lake Front
New Orleans, LA 70148
Phone: (504) 286-6556
Fax: (504) 286-7277

Earl K. Long Library—Archives and Manuscripts Division:
http://library.uno.edu/

Louisiana Military Records

More than 40 million Americans have participated in some time of war service since America was colonized. The chance of finding your ancestor amongst those records is exceptionally high. Military records can even reveal individuals who never actually served, such as those who registered for the two World Wars but were never called to duty.

Below are a number of links to websites and archives that contain Louisiana military records.

Louisiana State Archives – Confederate and Union military service records, bounty land claims, Confederate pension records, rosters, court martial records, and much more
3851 Essen Lane
P.O. Box 94125
Baton Rouge, LA 70804-9125
Tel: 225.922.1000
Fax: 225.922.0433

Louisiana State Archives :
http://www.sos.la.gov/HistoricalResources/ResearchHistoricalRecords/Pages/default.aspx

New Orleans Public Library's Louisiana Division & City Archives – Revolutionary War records, Florida War records, War of 1812 records, Civil War records, Spanish American War records, WWI records

219 Loyola Ave
New Orleans, LA 70112
Tel: 504-529-7323

New Orleans Public Library's Louisiana Division & City Archives: http://nutrias.org/guides/genguide/militaryrecords.htm

U.S. National Archives – WWI Draft registration cards, casualties lists, WWI and WWII service records, Korean War records, Vietnam War records, Civil War and Spanish-American War records, and casualties lists.

U.S. National Archives link to:
http://www.archives.gov/research/military/veterans/online.html

Family Search has the following indexes that can be searched online for free:

Louisiana Civil War Service Records of Confederate Soldiers, 1861-1865 : https://familysearch.org/search/collection/1932372

Louisiana, Civil War Service Records of Union Soldiers, 1861-1865: https://familysearch.org/search/collection/1932399

Louisiana Confederate Pensions, 1898-1950: https://familysearch.org/search/collection/1838535

Louisiana First Registration Draft Cards, 1940-1945: https://familysearch.org/search/collection/1916286

US Department of Veterans Affairs Nationwide Gravesite Locator – includes information on veterans and their family members buried in veterans and military cemeteries having a government grave marker.

US Department of Veterans Affairs Nationwide Gravesite Locator: http://gravelocator.cem.va.gov/

You may also find your ancestor's military records in the following databases:

United States Index to Indian Wars Pension Files, 1892-1926 – military pension records of soldiers who fought in the Indian Wars between 1817 and 1898

United States Index to Indian Wars Pension Files, 1892-1926: https://familysearch.org/search/collection/1979427

United States Registers of Enlistments in the U.S. Army, 1798-1914 - index of men who enlisted in the United States Army, 1798-1914.

United States Registers of Enlistments in the U.S. Army, 1798-1914: https://familysearch.org/search/collection/1880762

United States Mexican War Pension Index, 1887-1926 - index to Mexican War pension files for service between 1846 and 1848

United States Mexican War Pension Index, 1887-1926: https://familysearch.org/search/collection/1979390

Civil War Soldiers Service Records - Service records for both Union and Confederate soldiers indexed by soldier's name, rank, and unit.

Civil War Soldier Service Records: http://go.fold3.com/civilwar_records/

Louisiana Cemetery Records

As convenient as it is to search cemetery records online, keep in mind that there are a few disadvantages over visiting a cemetery in person. They are:

- Tombstone information is not always accurately transcribed
- The arrangement of the graves in a cemetery can be crucial as family members are often buried next to each other or in the same grave. This arrangement is not always preserved in the alphabetical indexes that are found online.

With that information in mind, the following websites have databases that can be searched online for Louisiana Cemetery records.

Louisiana Tombstone Transcription Project - death and burial records

Louisiana Tombstone Transcription Project:
http://www.usgwtombstones.org/louisiana/louisian.html

African American Cemeteries Online – African American, slave, and Native American cemetery records

African American Cemeteries Online:
http://africanamericancemeteries.com/ar/

Access Genealogy – huge database of Louisiana cemetery record transcriptions

Access Genealogy:
http://www.accessgenealogy.com/cemetery/louisiana-cemetery-records.htm

Find a Grave – over 100 million grave records can be searched on this site. Search can be conducted by name, location, or cemetery name.

Find a Grave: http://www.findagrave.com/

Interment.net - A free online database containing approximately 4 million cemetery records from around the world.

Interment.net: http://www.interment.net/

Billion Graves – as the name implies, you can search a billion records including headstone photos, transcriptions, cemetery records, and grave locations.

Billion Graves:
http://billiongraves.com/pages/search/index.php#cemetery

Louisiana Obituaries

Obituaries can reveal a wealth about our ancestor and other relatives. You can search our **Louisiana Newspaper Obituaries Listings** from hundreds of Louisiana newspapers online for free.

Louisiana Newspaper Obituaries Listings:
http://obituarieshelp.org/louisiana_newspaper_obituaries.html

Louisiana Wills and Probate Records

The documents found in a probate packet may include a complete inventory of a person's estate, newspaper entries, witness testimony, a copy of a will, list of debtors and creditors, names of executors or trustees, names of heirs. They can not only tell you about the ancestor you're currently researching, but lead to other ancestors.

In Louisiana these records must be accessed through the Louisiana District Courts, but some can be found online as well. You can obtain copies of the original probate records by writing to the **Louisiana Clerks of Court** in the relevant district.

Louisiana Clerks of Court:
http://laclerksofcourt.org/clerksofcourt.htm

In Louisiana there are several repositories and online indexes where wills and probate records and indexes to them can be viewed. They are:

New Orleans Notarial Archives – Searchable online index of notary records which include Slave emancipations, property records, bonds, slave sales records, wills, mortgages, estate records and many other notary records dating from 1735 to July 1970

Notarial Archives Division Research Center
1340 Poydras Street, Suite 360
New Orleans, LA 70112
Telephone: (504) 407-0106
Fax: (504) 680-9607

New Orleans Notarial Archives:
http://www.notarialarchives.org/research.htm

New Orleans Public Library's Louisiana Division & City Archives – huge database or probate records for Orleans Parish probates and wills records.

219 Loyola Ave
New Orleans, LA 70112
Tel: 504-529-7323

New Orleans Public Library's Louisiana Division & City Archives link to: http://nutrias.org/guides/genguide/civilcourt.htm

Family Search has the following indexes that can be searched online for free:

Louisiana Orleans Court Records, 1822-1880:
https://familysearch.org/search/collection/2030501

Louisiana Orleans Parish Second District Judicial Court Case Files, 1846-1880: https://familysearch.org/search/collection/1879925

Louisiana, Orleans Parish Will Books, 1805-1920:
https://familysearch.org/search/collection/2019728

Louisiana Immigration and Naturalization Records

The naturalization process generated many types of records, including petitions, declarations of intention, and oaths of allegiance. These records can provide family historians with information such as a person's birth date and place of birth, immigration year, marital status, spouse information, occupation, witnesses' names and addresses, and more.

Louisiana was an important entry point during the colonization of the United States, and many immigrants passed through the port of New Orleans.

New Orleans Public Library's Louisiana Division & City Archives – huge database or passenger lists, crews lists, customs records, and proofs of citizenship for the port of New Orleans, as well as Naturalization records from the Orleans Parish civil and criminal courts for the period 1828-1906 and from the federal court in New Orleans for the period 1811-1985

219 Loyola Ave
New Orleans, LA 70112
Tel: 504-529-7323

New Orleans Public Library's Louisiana Division & City Archives:
http://nutrias.org/guides/genguide/immigrationrecords.htm

The **U.S. National Archives** has passenger lists or indexes of American ports for 1820 to 1940, as well as immigration and naturalization records for the entire United States. These records can also be accessed at the **National Archives Regional Branch in Atlanta**

US National Archives:
http://www.archives.gov/research/immigration/passenger-arrival.html

National Archives Regional Branch in Atlanta:
http://www.archives.gov/atlanta/

Louisiana Native American Records

Access Genealogy – Louisiana Native American census records, tribal histories, and much more

Access Genealogy: http://www.accessgenealogy.com/native/louisiana-indian-tribes.htm

U.S. National Archives - information on American Indians who maintained their ties to Federally-recognized Tribes (1830-1970).

U.S. National Archives: http://www.archives.gov/research/native-americans/

Records of the Bureau of Indian Affairs (BIA)

Records of the Bureau of Indian Affairs (BIA): http://www.archives.gov/research/guide-fed-records/groups/075.html

American Indians Records Repository - records dating from the 1700s including trust, education and other historic Indian Affairs records

American Indian Records Repository
Meritex Enterprises
17501 West 98th Street
Lenexa, KS 66219
Phone: 913-888-0601

American Indians Records Repository: http://www.doi.gov/ost/records_mgmt/american-indian-records-repository.cfm

Missing Matriarchs – Resources for Researching Female Louisiana Ancestors

Looking for female ancestors requires an adjustment of how we view traditional records sources. A woman's identity was often under that of her husband, and often individual records for them can be difficult to locate. The following resources are effective in locating female ancestors in Louisiana where traditional records may not reveal them.

<u>Bibliographies</u>

1. *French and Spanish Records of Louisiana: A Bibliographical Guide to Archives and Manuscript Sources,* Henry Putney Beers (Louisiana State University Press, 1989)
2. *Women and New Orleans: A History,* Mary Geham (Margaret Media, 1988)
3. *The New Orleans Guide to Collections on Women,* Susan Tucker (Tulane University, 1989)

Selected Resources for Louisiana Women's History

Hill Memorial Library
Louisiana State University
Baton Rouge, LA 70803

The Newcomb Archives
Newcomb College Institute of Tulane University
Contact: Susan Tucker
Caroline Richardson Building
62 Newcomb Place, #203
New Orleans, LA 70118
Tel: 504-865-5239
Email: susannah@tulane.edu

New Orleans Public Library
Louisiana Division
219 Loyola Ave.
New Orleans, LA 70140

Common Louisiana Surnames

The following surnames are among the most common in Louisiana and are also being currently researched by other genealogists. If you find your surname here, there is a chance that some research has already been performed on your ancestor.

AIME, ADAMS, ALLAIN, ALLY, ALLEMAND, ALLISON, ALSANDOR, ALCINDOR, AMAT, AMAUD, AMEDEE, AMIRATI, ARSCENEAUX, ARCHIE, ARMONT(d) , AYBRY, AUGUST, AVRILLE, BACQUIE, BAHAM, BAPTISTE, BARBARIN, BARRETT, BASQUEZ, BATIER, BAYON, BEAUREGARD, BECNEL, BELHOMME, BELL, BENOIT, BERGERON, BERIDON, BERLECHEAU, BERNARD, BERTON, BERTRAND, BLACHE, BLANBIN, BLOOM, BOCAGE, BOSSIERRE, BORAS, BORSKI, BOUDREAUX, BONEE, BORDENAVE, BOUCREE, BOUGERE, BOUTTE, BRAUD, BREAUX, BRIDAY, BRICOUD, BROUSSARD, BROYARD, BRUNEL, BUSH, BUSTAMENTE, BUJEAU, CAZENAVE, CAMP, CARMOUCHE, CHAISSON, CHAMPAGNE, CHARLES, CHENEVERT, CHESSE, CHEVAL, CHAVALIER, CHRISTOPHE, COFFEY, COLLINS, COMEAUX, CONDOLL, CORBERT, CORBET, COIBERT, CORBETTE, COULON, COURTADE, COUSIN, COUSTANT, CRAIG, CROCKER, DAIGLE, DALFERES, DARCANTEL, DARENSBOURG, DAUPHIN, DAUTERIVE, DAVE, DAVID, DAVIS, DEGRUY, DELAHOSSAY, DESARZANT, DECUIR, DESLANDES, DESSALLES, DEVEZIN, DEVILLE, DOBARD, DOMINQUE, DOUCET, DOUCETTE, DUBOURG, DUFFEL, DUPONT, DUTREUIL, DUVAL, DIAS, DEMAZILLIERE, DOBARD, DREUX, DUBREUIL, DUBUCLET, DUGAS, DUMING, DUPAIN, DUPLANTIER, DUPONT, EBERT, EDWARDS, ELLSWORTH, ESTORGE, EWELL, FERNANDEZ, FERRAND, FETTE, FIETEL, FLETCHER, FLOT, FONTENETTE, FONTRNOT, FORSTALL, FORTIER, FOSTER, FOULONE, FOULON, FRANCIS, FRANCOISE, FRICK, GABRIEL, GALBRETH, GALLE, GARCIA, GLAPION, GARNIER, GAUTHIER, GAY, GAYAUT, GUILLOT, GALLOT, GEDDRY, GYRON, GODEAU, GORDON, GOUDEAU, GRANT, GRAVES, GREEN,

GUIDRY, GUILLACOME, GUILLORY, GUYAL, HARRIS, HART, HAINS, HARLEAUX, HASTINGS, HAYDEL, HEISSER, HENNET DIT SASCHAGRIN, HERBERT, HEBERT, HIRSCH, HODGE, HONORE DIT DESTREHAN, HUBBARD, HUGON, JACKSON, JAMES, JORDOIN, JARREAU, JEANJACQUES, JEANNE, JEFFRION, JETER, JOLIVERE, JONES, JOSEPH, JOUBERT, JUGE, JULES, KINDLER, LABAT, LABOT, LABEAU, LABO, LABEAUD, LAVEAU, L'HERISSE, LABOSTRIE, LACOUR, LACROIX, LADMIRAULT, LADNIER, LAFRERE, LAGARDE, LAGAUX, LALANDE, LALONIER, LANDRY, LAMOTHE, LOMOTTE, LASTRATES, LAURANT, LAVEAU(X), LEBLANC, LEBEAU, LECLAIRE(C), LEDE, LEDET, LEDAY, LEDEE, LEDUFF, LEFEBVRE, LEFRERE, LEGENDRE, LEGER, LEGGETT, LEJEUNE, LE'OBIA, LEOBIA, LEOBIE, LETORY, LORREINS, MAGNON, MAIGNET, MARANT, MARCELLE, MARCELL, MARCHAND, MARTEL, MARIGNY, MATEOS, MATHE, MATHER, MAETHER, MATHIEU, MAUK, MAUCK, MANK, MAURICE, MAURY, MAVEAUX, MAYEAUX, MAXENT, MAZET, MCCARTHY, MCCUE, MEILLEUR, MENDOZA, MERRITT, METEYE, MILLER, MILLOT, MOMTREUIL, MONIER, MEUNIER, MONROE, MONTEILH, MONTGOMERY, MOORE, MORET, MOUTON, MUJOR, MUSE, NABA, NACOSTE, NELSON, NICHOLAS, OFFRAY, OLIVER, OLIVIER, ORY, OZENNE, PAPILLION, PASCAL, PATIN, PELLERIN, PELLESSIER, PEREZ, PERRAULT, PERALT, PHILIPPI, PHILLIPS, PHICHON, PIERRE, PIZERO, PLEASANT, PLAISSANCE, PLICQUE, PLOUNT, POIRRIER, POPULUS, PORCHE, POREE, PORTER POTTER, POURCIAU, POYDRAS, PRADIER, PRADIA, PRADE, PRILLION, RABY, RAMOND, RAMON, RANDOLPH, RATLEFF, RAYMOND, REINE, REYNAUD, REYNES, RICARD, RICHARD, RICKET, RIDEAU, RIPOLL, ROBERT,

ROBERTSON, ROBINSON, ROGERS, ROMAN, RONDENO, ROUSSEAU, ROYAL, ROQUES, SAUCIER, SAINT LOUIS, SCOTT, SERF, SHEDRICK, SHEFFIELD, SIGG, SIMEON, SIMIEN, SIMON SORAPURU, SOULE, ST. AMANT, ST. ANDRE, ST. ANDREW, ST. CYR, STANLEY, TACHERT, TAYLOR, TERNOIR, THOMAS, THRUHILE, TIRCUIT, TOUNOIR, TOUSSAINT, TREGRE, TREVIGNE, TROULLIER, TUREAUD, TURNOIR, TOUNOIR, VENTRESS, VEROT, VIGNAUD, VIGNE, VILLAVASSO, VAUCRESSON, WALKER, WEBB, WELSH, WALSH, WHILLEY, WILEY, WILLIAMS, WILLOZ, WILTZ, XAVIER, ZENON, ZENO

About the Author

Gary L. Morris worked from 2009 to 2014 as a professional researcher for a major player in the genealogy field. After tracing his family lineage back to 1683, he has decided to publish these helpful guides to share the valuable information he has discovered during his career to help others trace their family lineages. An avid genealogist himself, he hopes you will find this guide factual, thorough, helpful, and most of all, effective in helping you to find your family members.